Space Sailors

Aurora Colón García

Contents

Rigby

A Harcourt Achieve Imprint

www.Rigby.com
1-800-531-5015

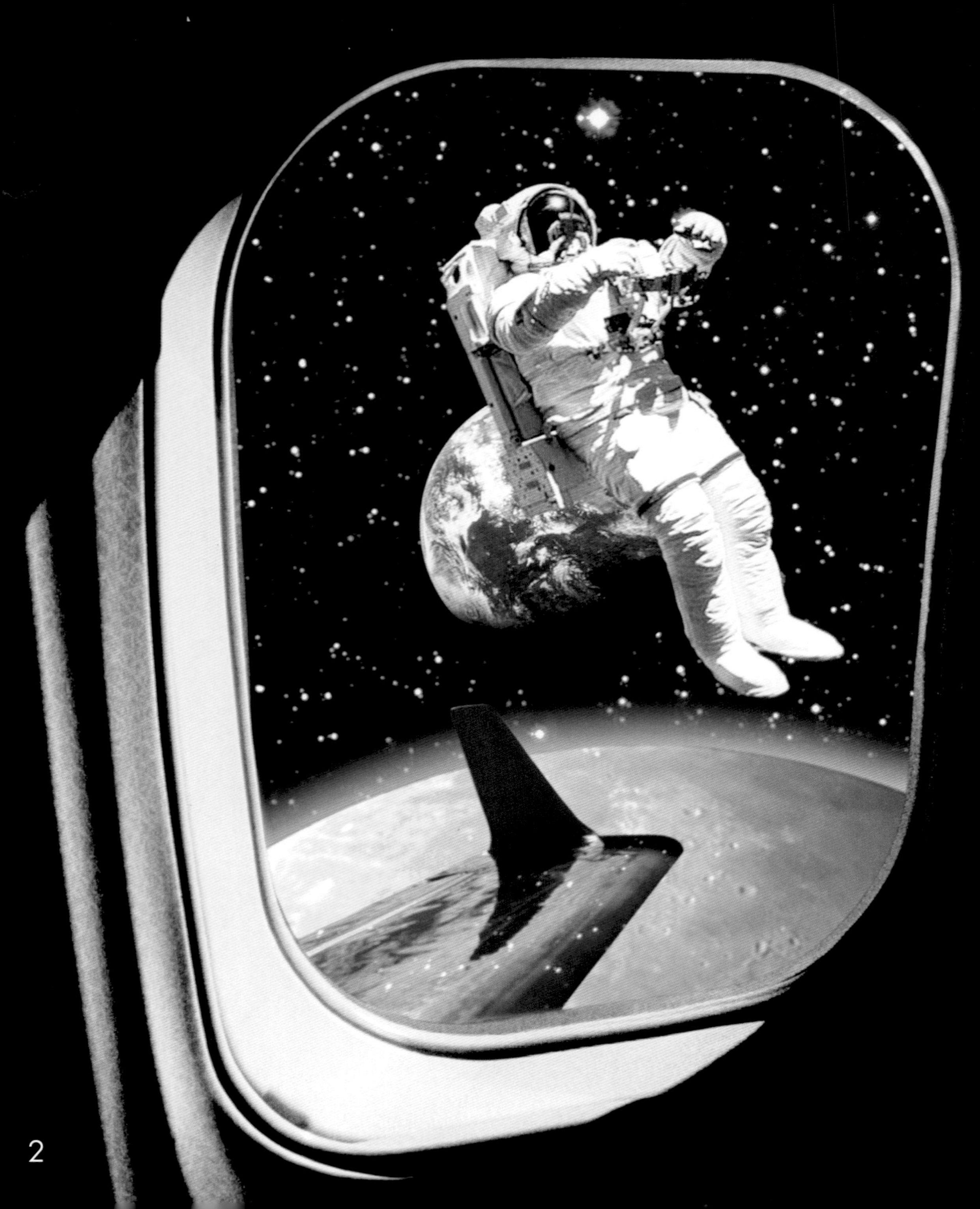

Would you like to be a space sailor?
A space sailor is an astronaut.
Astronaut means
"sailor among the stars."

Astronauts ask many questions.
They need to know
about science and math.
They need to know many things
about space.

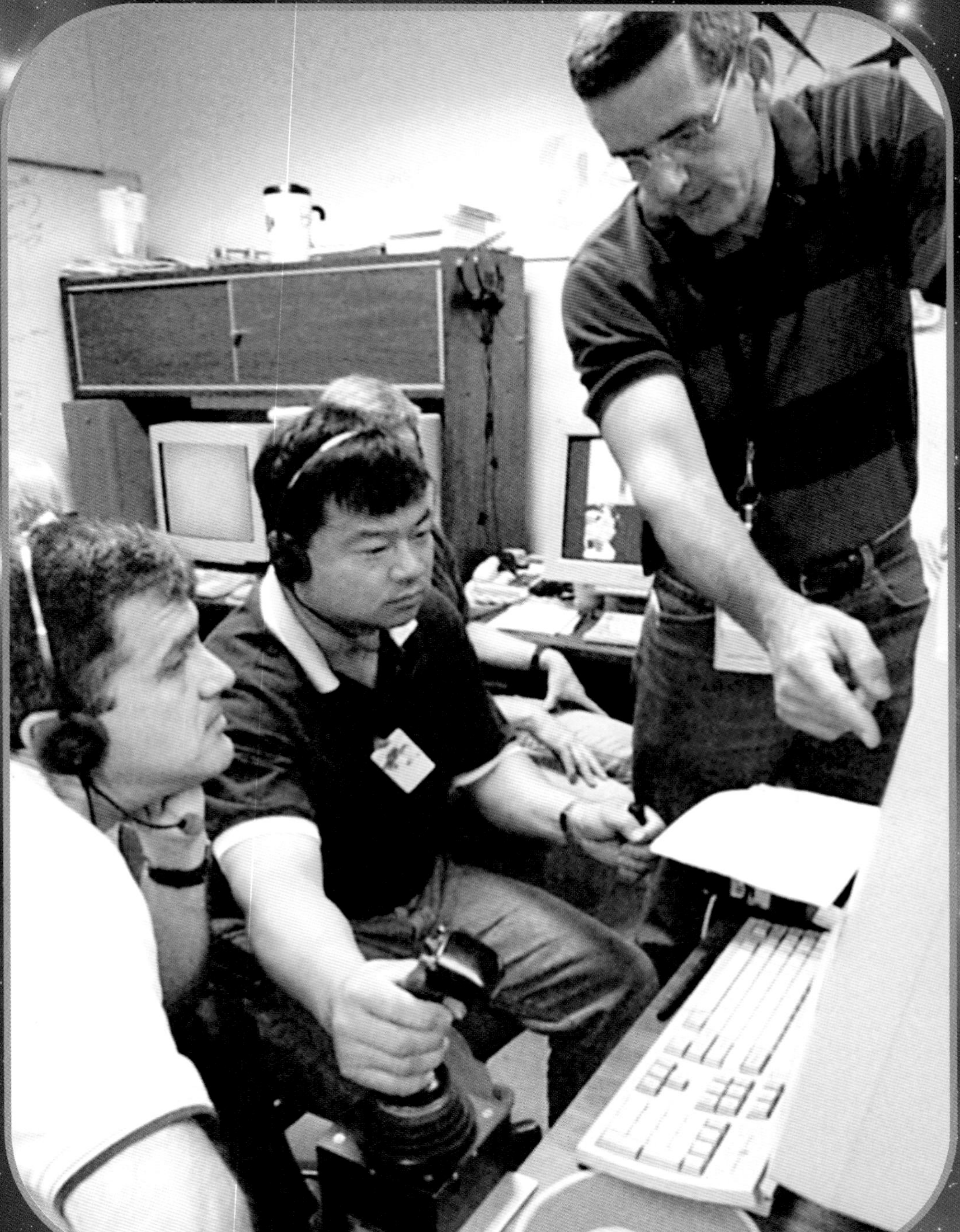

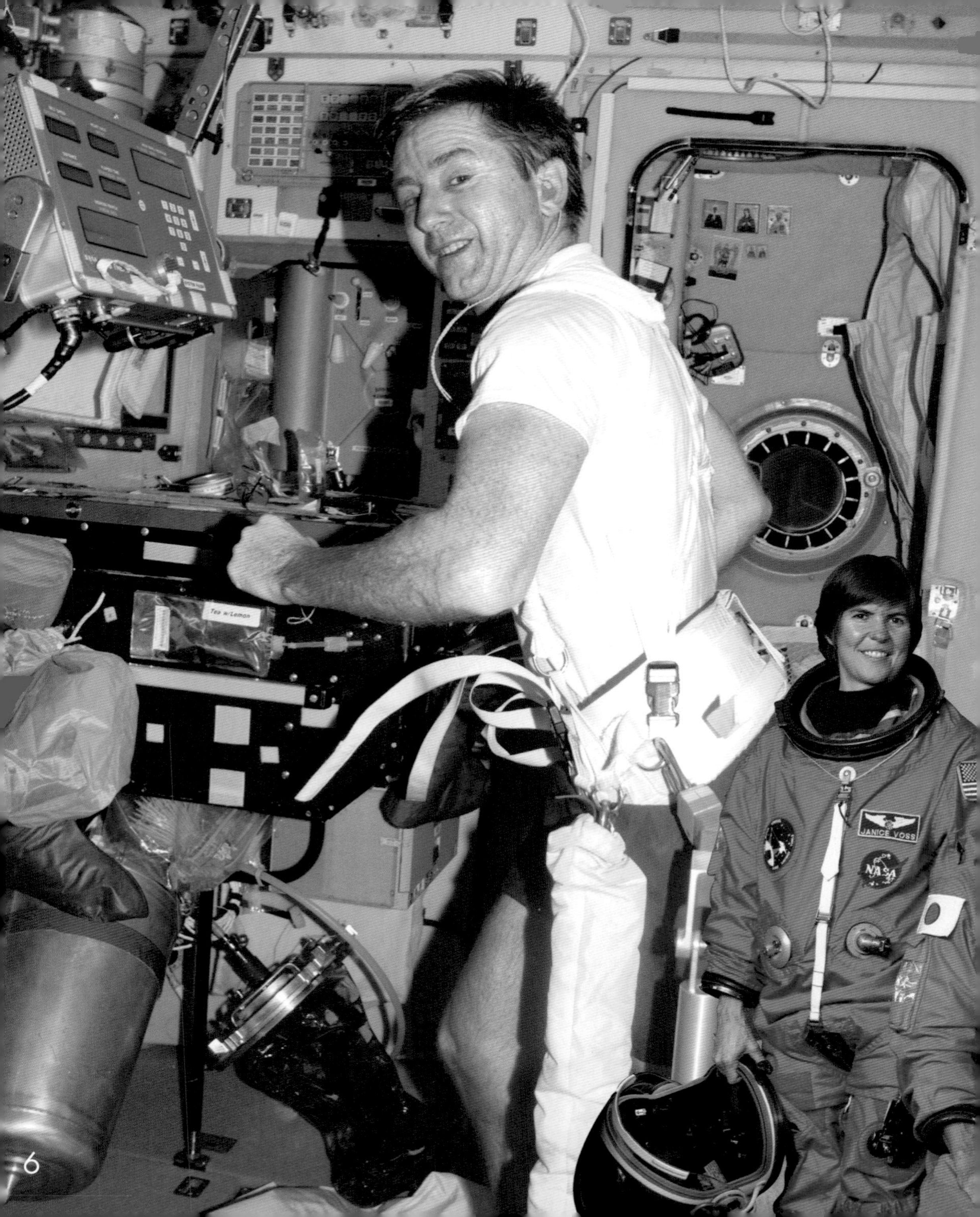
Tea w/Lemon
JANICE VOSS
NASA

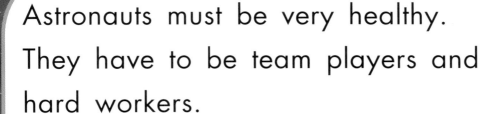

Astronauts must be very healthy.
They have to be team players and hard workers.
Astronauts must go to college and study, study, study!

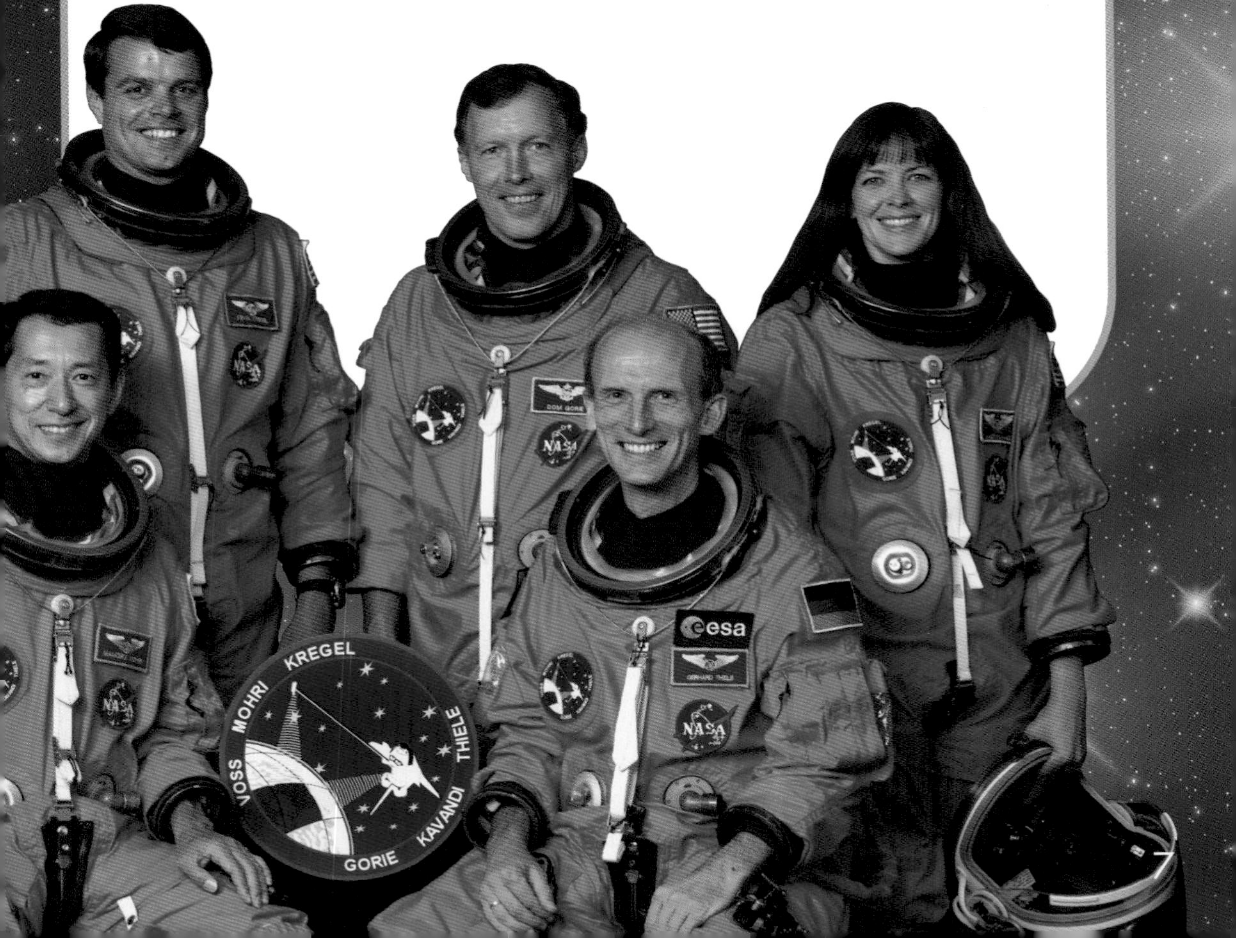
KREGEL
MOHRI
VOSS
GORIE
KAVANDI
THIELE
esa

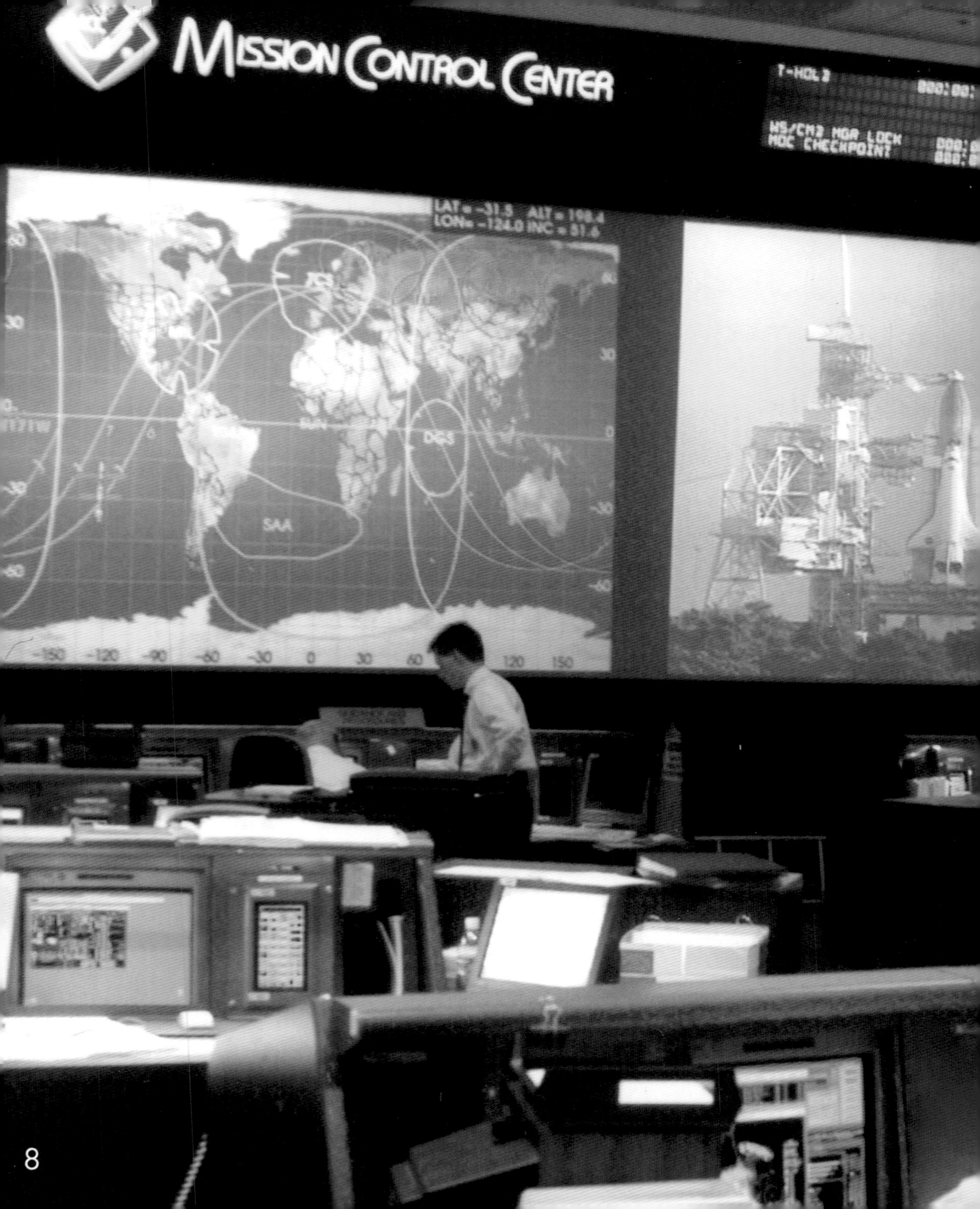

MISSION CONTROL CENTER
LAT = -31.5 ALT = 198.4
LON= -124.0 INC = 51.6
SAA

The Johnson Space Center
in Houston, Texas, trains astronauts.
It costs about 10 million dollars
to train an astronaut.

Training to be an astronaut is
very hard work.
There are many jobs
that an astronaut must learn to do.

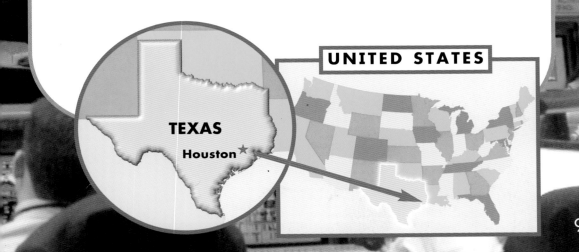

TEXAS

Houston

UNITED STATES

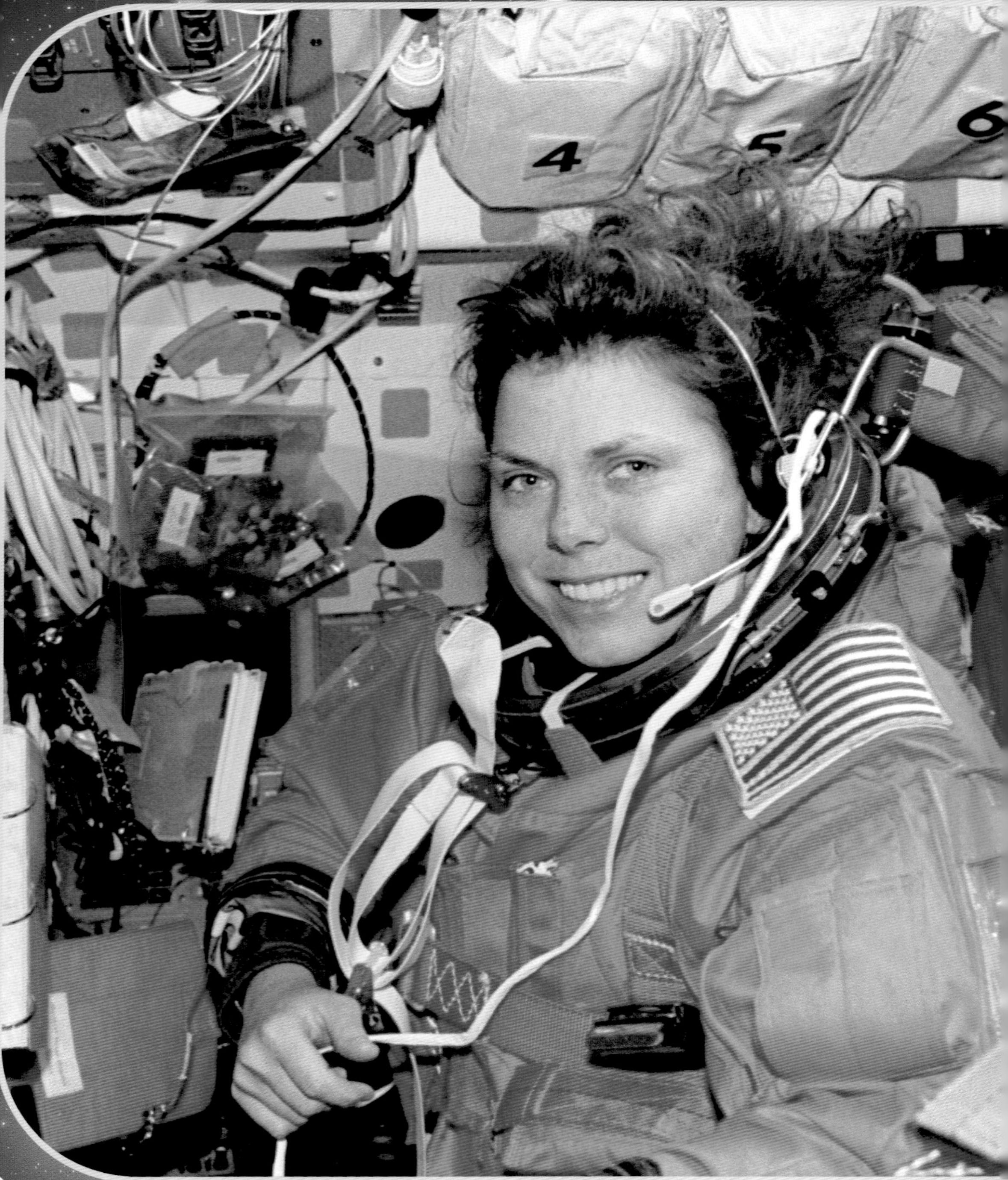
4

Astronauts train in special labs
at the Johnson Space Center.
Astronauts learn to live and
work in space.
They learn to use buttons
that control the spacecraft.

Astronauts learn to move in space suits by going underwater. Moving underwater feels like floating in space.

The astronauts need a lot of practice to get used to it.

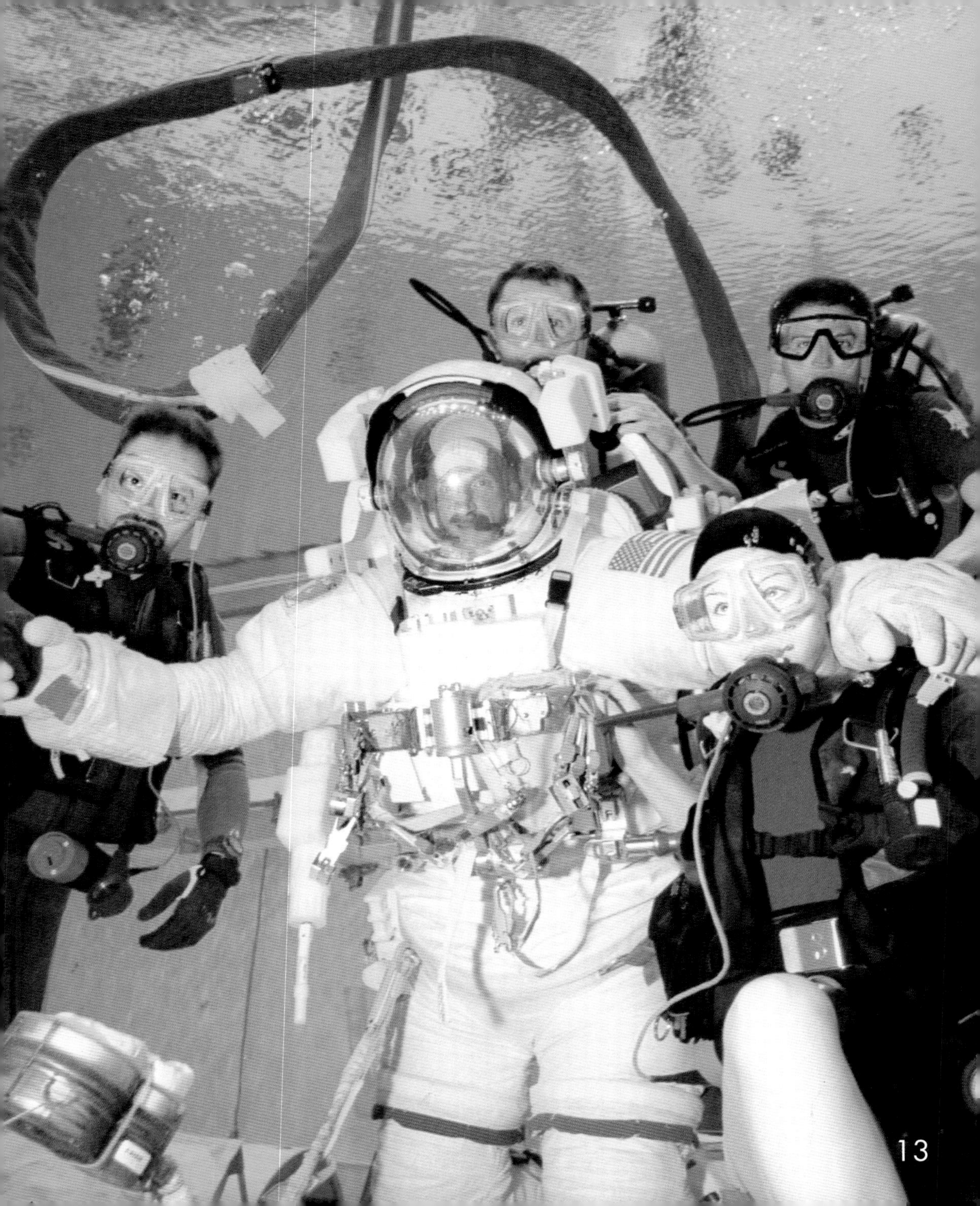

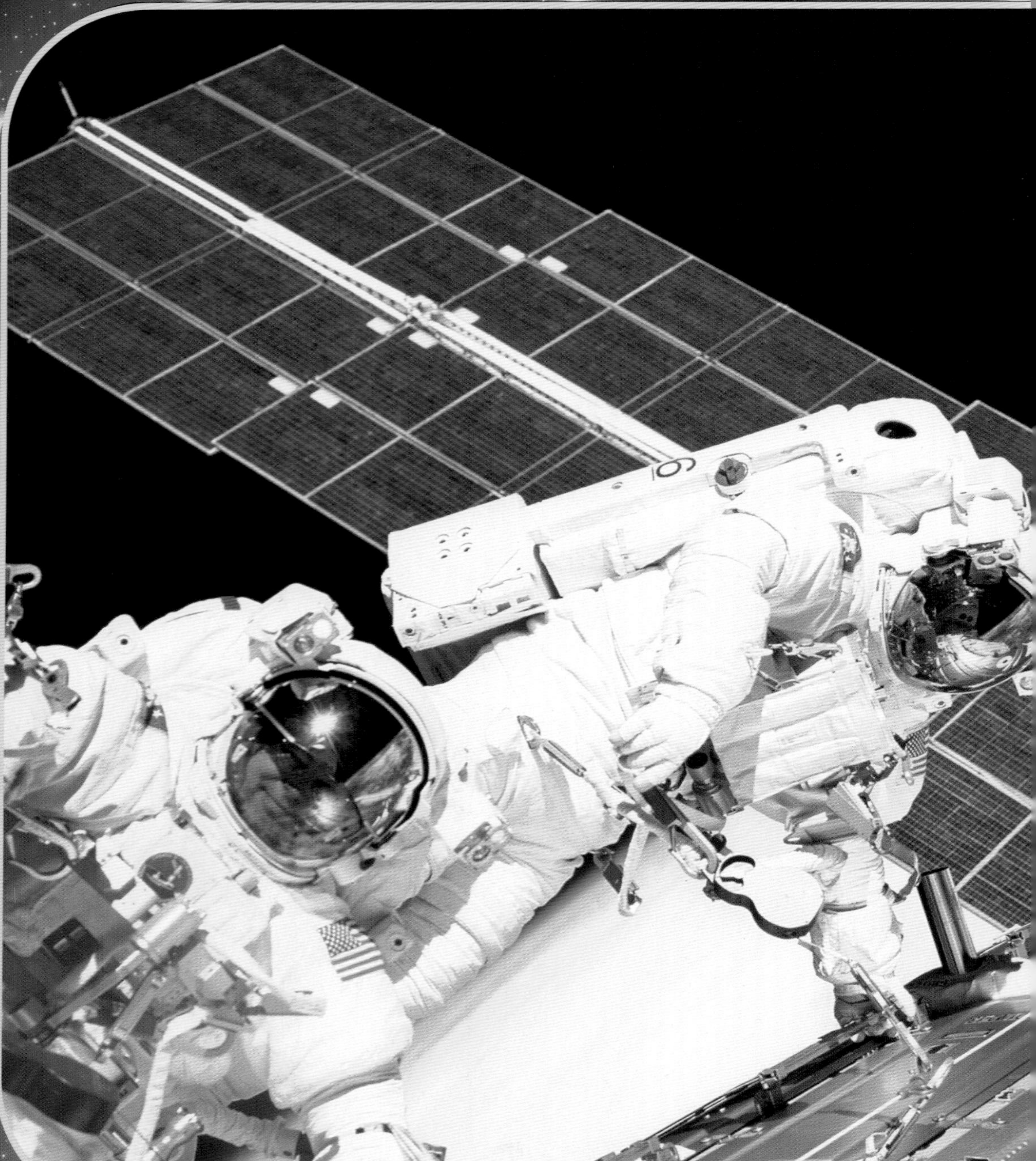

Astronauts train to be part of a team. Each team player has a special job to do.

They do science experiments and learn to fix things in space.

Astronauts learn to solve problems together.

The world has a lot more to learn
about space travel.
Being an astronaut is
a great adventure!